Have Fun With
Panjabi

This book is dedicated to Baby Jaipal, Baby Reeya & Baby Aneel

Author: Kiran Lyall
Art Director & Illustrations: Venisha Sudra

Have Fun With Panjabi

First published May 2010 by Buzzword UK
On behalf of Sweet Lyall Ltd
www.sweetlyall.com

Printed in the UK.

ISBN: 978-1-902544-07-6

A CIP catalogue record for this book is available from the British Library.

Panjabi is also commonly referred to as Punjabi, and like every language around the world is spoken with a different accent depending on locality. In this book, the Panjabi words containing two or more syllables, have been separated by dots to assist with pronunciation.

Foreword

Panjabi youngsters of yesteryear's diaspora grew up listening to their elders speak to them in Panjabi, and they responded either in confident or broken Panjabi, or simply English. Constructing sentences for some may have been an arduous task, yet in all three cases, the comprehension of the language was ensured. As Panjabi youth born and reared in English-speaking countries grew up and married, the language of communication between the spouses remained English. And unless Panjabi-speaking elders are in close and regular contact, the next generation is left with limited auditory access to Panjabi and therefore next to no comprehension. Thus, fresh material presupposing no knowledge of Panjabi is now needed to educate a new wave of Panjabi children if the language is to survive outside of Panjab; Kiran Lyall's 'Have fun with Panjabi' assists in serving such a purpose.

To overcome the use of native scripts, she has employed the Roman one for transliteration based on a principle of 'say what you see'. Because this way of transliterating is subjective by nature, the Panjabi words in this book have been tried and tested on Panjabi children and non-Panjabi adults, with the spellings continually modified until what is uttered is a close-to-accurate pronunciation. This is, of course, no substitute for learning the original script which is most suited for the language in question. But at the early stages of making a child's acquaintance with Panjabi, this book allows those who are unfamiliar with the script to at least access the Panjabi language in order to enable their children to do so.

If parents are using this book with their children, it uses their own knowledge of the words and their accurate pronunciation. If those with no knowledge of Panjabi are using this to help build their own vocabulary, having a native speaker of the language check the learner's pronunciation is invaluable. I mention this to bring about caution concerning certain Panjabi sounds which employ only one grapheme in the Roman script. These are primarily t and d which can be used for retroflex sounds such as topi (hat) and dabba (box), and dental sounds such as those in tabla (Indian hand drums) and daal (lentils). Ideally, I would hope that the learner would one day come to learn the native script for better acquisition of Panjabi, but until then, such a book ensures that the language is not altogether lost. For that purpose, I commend such an endeavour.

Rishi Handa BSc (Hons) MA (Lond)

Rishi Handa is a school teacher of Mathematics, Religion and Philosophy, and also teaches a number of South Asian languages. He teaches Panjabi at the School of Oriental and African Studies (SOAS), University of London and is an examiner for Panjabi at King's College London.

Counting

Gin·tee

One
Ik

Two
Dho

Three
Tinn

Four
Chaar

Five
Panj

Six
Cheh

Seven
Saht

Eight
Aaht

Nine
Noh

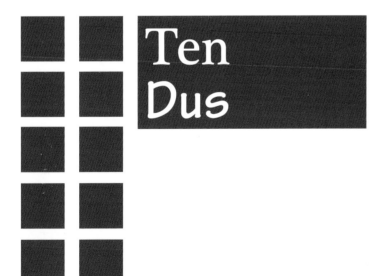

Ten
Dus

11 Eleven *Gee·ya·ra*	**19** Nineteen *Oo·nee*	**27** Twenty seven *Sat·ta·ee*
12 Twelve *Baa·raa*	**20** Twenty *Vee*	**28** Twenty eight *Aat·ta·ee*
13 Thirteen *Teh·ra*	**21** Twenty one *Ik·kee*	**29** Twenty nine *Oo·na·tee*
14 Fourteen *Choh·da*	**22** Twenty two *Baa·ee*	**30** Thirty *Tee*
15 Fifteen *Pun·dra*	**23** Twenty three *Tay·ee*	**35** Thirty five *Pen·tee*
16 Sixteen *Soh·la*	**24** Twenty four *Choh·vee*	**40** Forty *Cha·lee*
17 Seventeen *Sa·ta·ra*	**25** Twenty five *Pach·ee*	**50** Fifty *Paj·jah*
18 Eighteen *Aa·ta·ra*	**26** Twenty six *Chab·bee*	**100** One Hundred *Ik Soh*

Colours Rung

Red
Laal

Plural: Laal

Yellow
Pee·la

Plural: Pee·leh

Green
Har·ra
Plural: Har·reh

Blue
Nee·la
Plural: Nee·leh

17

Black
Kaa·la
Plural: Kaa·leh

White
Chit·ta
Plural: Chit·teh

Pink
Gu·la·bee

Plural: Gu·la·bee·ya

Purple
Jah·mu·nee

Plural: Jah·mu·nee

19

Fruit & Vegetables
Phal & Sab·jee

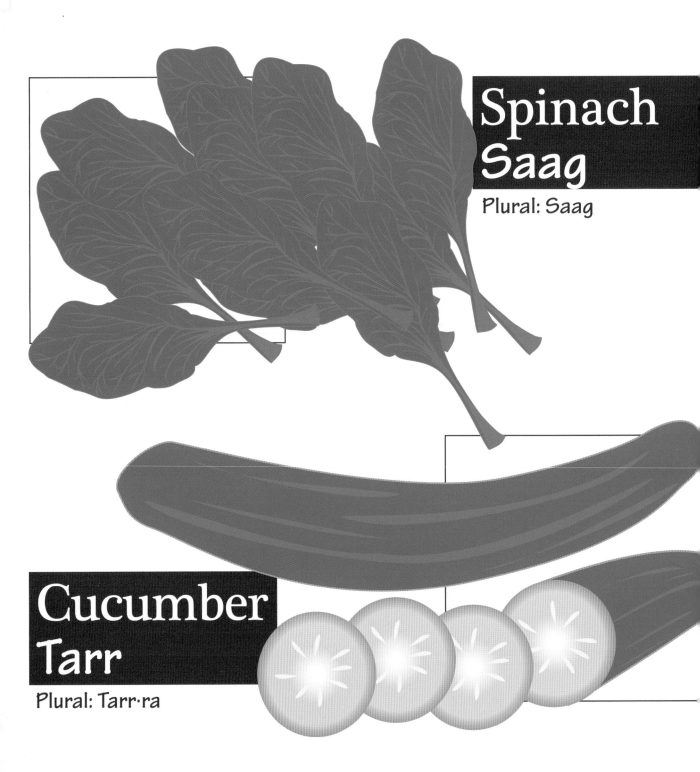

Spinach
Saag
Plural: Saag

Cucumber
Tarr
Plural: Tarr·ra

Onion
Gat·tah

Plural: Gat·teh

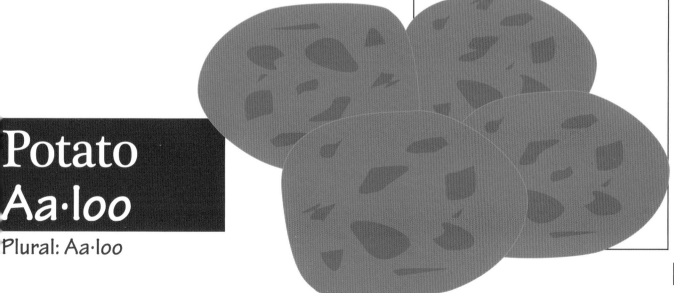

Potato
Aa·loo

Plural: Aa·loo

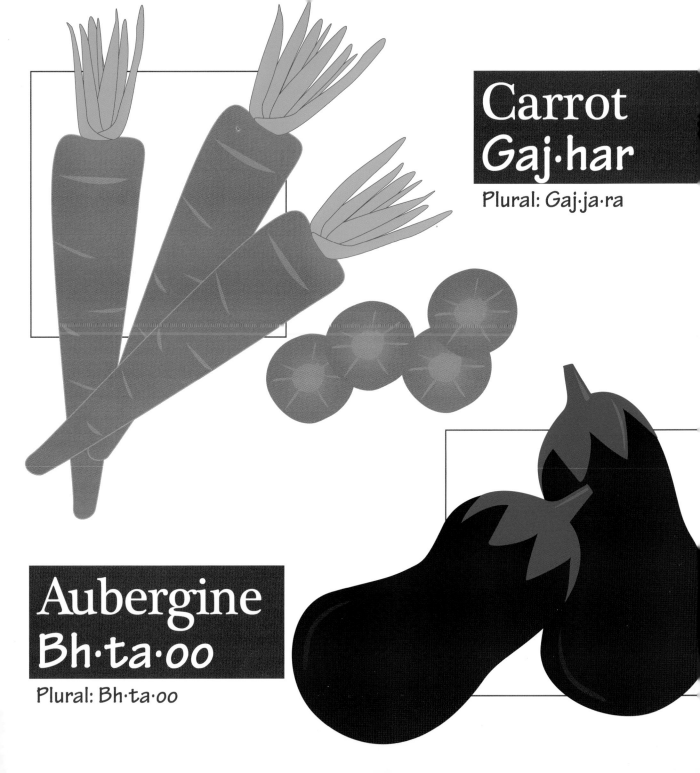

Carrot
Gaj·har
Plural: Gaj·ja·ra

Aubergine
Bh·ta·oo
Plural: Bh·ta·oo

Courgette
Ram Toh·ree
Plural: Ram Toh·ree·ya

Cauliflower
Go·bee
Plural: *Go·bee·ya*

25

Tomato
Tom·ma·tar
Plural: Tom·ma·tar

Pea
Mut·tar
Plural: Mut·tar

Garlic
Lus·san

Plural: Lus·san

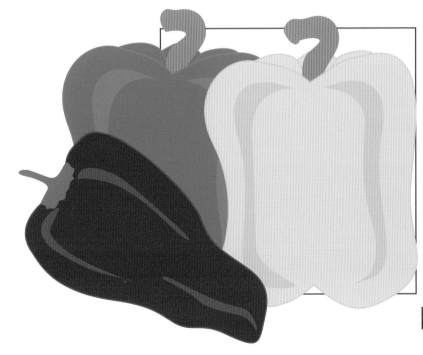

Pepper
Mir·ch

Plural: Mir·cha

Apple
Sehb
Plural: Sehb

Orange
San·tar·ra
Plural: San·tar·reh

Banana
Keh·la

Plural: Keh·leh

Grape
Un·goor

Plural: Un·goor

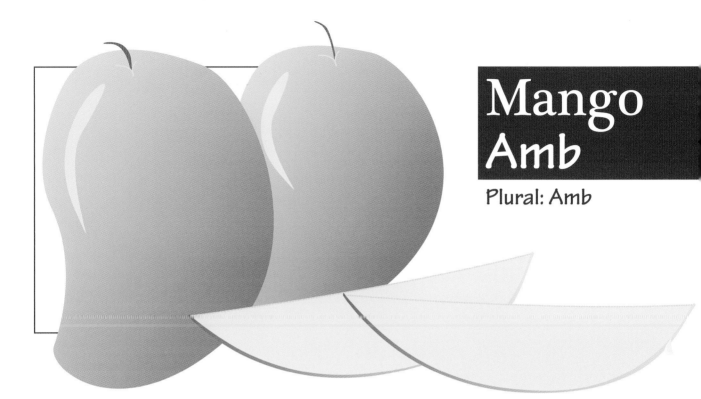

Mango
Amb

Plural: Amb

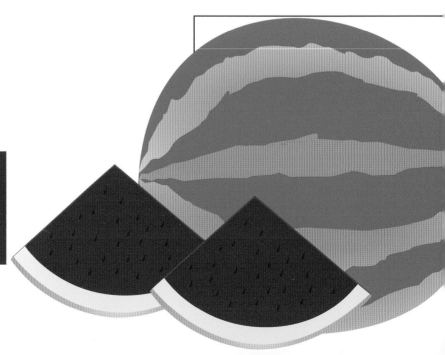

Melon
Kar·boo·ja

Plural: Kar·boo·jeh

Pomegranate
An·naar

Plural: An·naar

Lemon
Nim·boo

Plural: Nim·boo

31

What have you learnt?

- ✓ Gin·tee
- ✓ Rung
- ✓ Phal
- ✓ Sab·jee

One Red Onion
Ik Laal Gat·tah

1

Two Cauliflowers
Dho Go·bee·ya

Three Peppers
Tinn Mir·cha

3

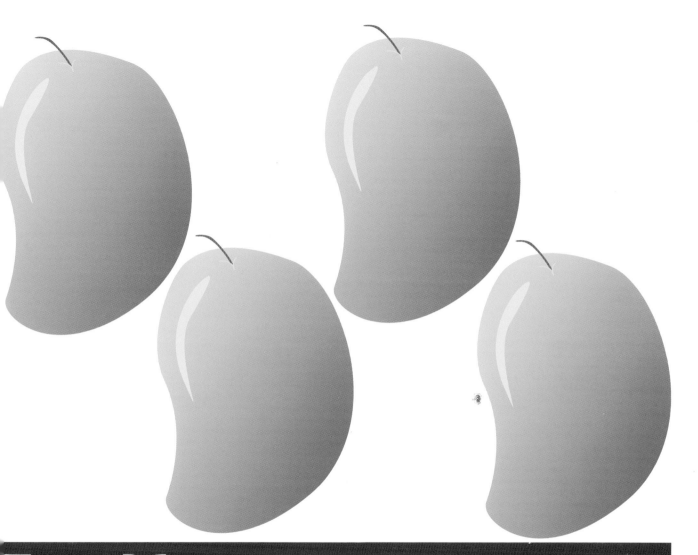

Four Mangoes
Chaar Amb

4

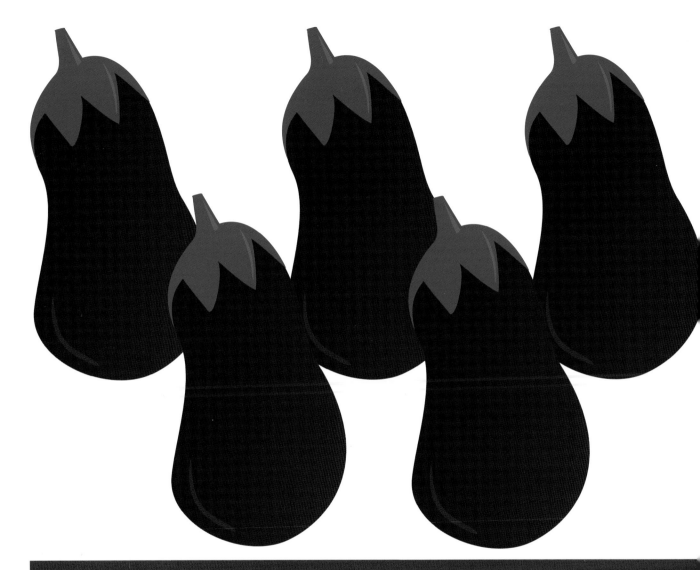

Five Purple Aubergines
Panj Jah·mu·nee Bh·ta·oo

5

Six Bananas
Cheh Keh·leh

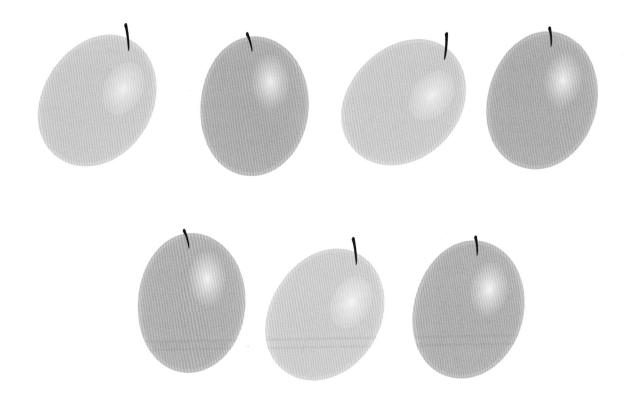

Seven Green Grapes
Saht Har·reh Un·goor

7

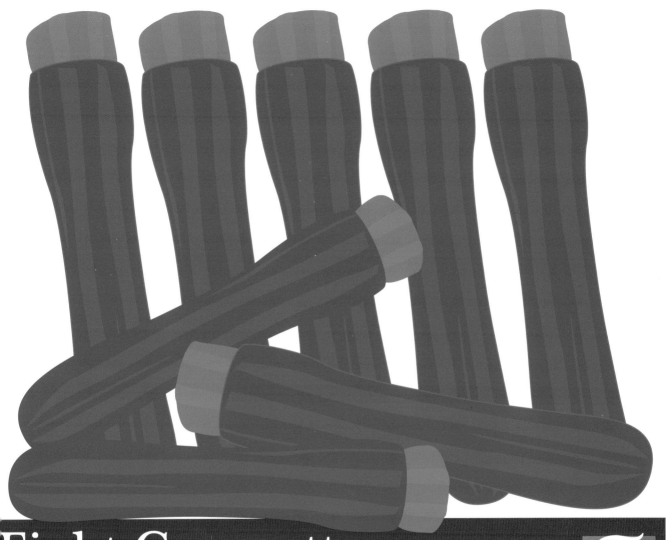

Eight Courgettes
Aaht Ram Toh·ree·ya

Nine Red Apples
Noh Laal Sehb

9

Ten Melons
Dus Kar·boo·jeh

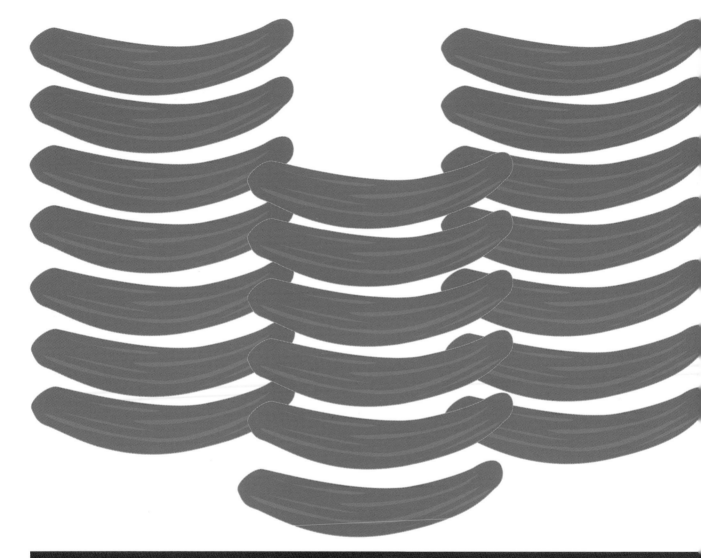

Twenty Cucumbers
Vee Tarr·ra

20

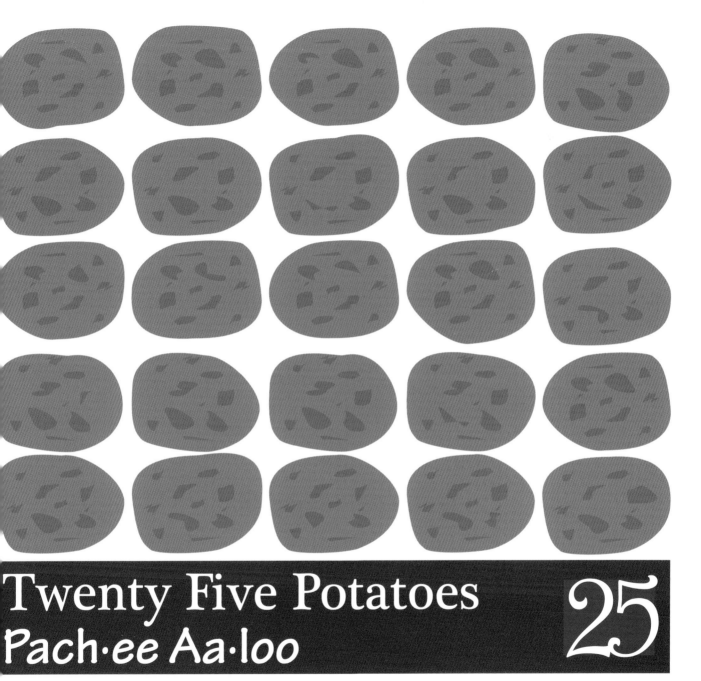

Twenty Five Potatoes
Pach·ee Aa·loo

25

Drinks

Water
Paa·nee

Juice (of a fruit)
Rus

Tea
Chaa

Milk

Milk
Dudh

Days of the Week

Haf·teh deh din

nday

Saturday

Monday
Sohm·vaar

Tuesday
Mun·gul·vaar

Wednesday
Budh·vaar

Thursday
Veer·vaar

Friday
Shoo·kar·vaar

Saturday
Sh·nich·char·vaar

Sunday
Eht·vaar

Friday

Saturday

Thursday

Sunday

Tuesday

Wednesday

Monday

53

The Author

Kiran's passion for the Panjabi language began as a child on her travels to India. Her annual holidays were normally spent with her grandma in Ambala or traveling around the Panjab and Mumbai. Kiran became fluent in Panjabi at a young age due to her parents strong influence, family connection with India and love for Panjabi bhangra music. Eventually aged 9, she decided to learn Panjabi the traditional way using script.

Now a mother, Kiran recently noticed that there is a lack of books available for English speaking parents who want their children to speak and explore the Panjabi language at home. She is hoping that the 'Have Fun With…' series will fill the gap and encourage young children to learn their mother tongue.

Acknowledgements

Firstly, I would like to thank all of the children who were involved in the research of this book and being the ultimate inspiration. I would also like to thank the following people for their help and advice: my mother – Bimla, Dev Lyall, Priya Lyall, Manjit Thai-jee, John Hughes of Buzzword UK, the Manor Creative team, Rajan Kalha, Simran and Harpal Khambay, Hans Raj and Vidya Sian, Gillian Stenhouse, Rimpy Rooprai, Kushty Sharda, Harps Hansra, Pardeep Chaggar, Baby Jaipal and most importantly, my husband Hardeep, for all his support and patience!

BOOK TWO COMING SOON
Please refer to www.sweetlyall.com for further information

Have Fun With The Environment This book is printed using vegetable based inks on paper from well managed sources.